Flower Therapy Journal

Flower Therapy Journal

A Prescription and Guide for Self-Care & Living Your Life in Full Bloom

Andrea M. Zeddies, PhD

Tampa, Florida

The content associated with this book is the sole work and responsibility of the author. Gatekeeper Press had no involvement in the generation of this content.

Flower Therapy Journal: A Prescription and Guide for Self-Care & Living Your Life in Full Bloom

Published by Gatekeeper Press
7853 Gunn Hwy., Suite 209
Tampa, FL 33626
www.GatekeeperPress.com

Cover image: iStockphoto.com/Seamless Pattern Emporium

Book illustrations were generated by an Artificial Intelligence (AI) system through Shutterstock.

ISBN (paperback): 9781662946516
eISBN: 9781662946523

Contents

Introduction ... vii

January Flower: Carnation ... 1
February Flower: Violet ... 8
March Flower: Daffodil ... 15
April Flower: Daisy ... 22
May Flower: Lily of the Valley ... 29
June Flower: Rose ... 36
July Flower: Larkspur ... 43
August Flower: Gladiolus ... 50
September Flower: Aster ... 57
October Flower: Marigold ... 64
November Flower: Chrysanthemum ... 71
December Flower: Ranunculus ... 78

About the Author ... 85

Introduction

Many people are searching for a "prescription" for a happy life. Philosophers, intellects, psychologists, and researchers have scoured historical texts, spent hours pondering the meaning of life, and have attempted to solve the puzzle or at least come closer to an answer to these questions: What is our purpose? Why are we here? What am I meant to do with this one precious life?

Although no definitive answers exist, experts can agree on one thing: Enjoying the present moment is one of the keys to happiness. It's really all we have, because we can't predict the future, and it can be unhealthy and fruitless to live in the past. This is not to say that understanding one's past through therapy or other means is not productive or doesn't provide meaningful information to inform future decisions. Similarly, having healthy, measurable goals for one's future is a great way to set yourself up for success.

A philosophy and practice called "mindfulness" includes documented anecdotal and research evidence supporting its efficacy for boosting mood, decreasing anxiety, and improving one's outlook and overall health. The idea of mindfulness was cultivated in ancient Eastern philosophies about 2500 years ago and has been influential in Western scientific-based research and practices such as "mindfulness-based stress reduction," developed by Jon Kabat-Zinn, PhD, a professor of Medicine at Harvard University.[1]

Mindfulness is the awareness of the present moment without judgment, combined with loving-kindness towards oneself. The purpose of this practice is not to become numb to one's experience,

---

[1] Kabat-Zinn, J. (2003), Mindfulness-Based Stress Reduction, Constructivism in the Human Sciences, Vol. 8 (2), p. 73-107.

but rather to "wake up" and become more aware of your experience, using all of your senses to enhance your attention and heighten consciousness. You might argue that in this day and age, your mind is preoccupied and swirling with thoughts about world conflict, politics, worries about safety, providing for yourself and your family, and managing the intricacies of your daily life. One might imagine that this leaves little room for pausing to engage in anything "extra," much less a "time-consuming" practice such as mindfulness. The beauty of this practice is that you can employ it in any place at any time—the line at the grocery store, in your car during a traffic jam (As long as you pay attention to traffic!), while doing the dishes, or while eating a meal. You can engage in a regular practice for ten or twenty minutes a day, but even a few minutes of pausing and disengaging with electronics creates an opportunity to escape from the heightened hustle and bustle of everyday life.

Mindfulness involves noticing the sights, sounds, smells, touch, and/or tastes in your environment, while maintaining a neutral and nonjudgmental stance towards yourself. During your practice, if a challenging feeling arises—such as sadness, anger, anxiety, physical pain, or even despair—observe the feeling, acknowledge its presence (e.g. "there's that feeling again"), notice where in your body you feel that emotion or sensation (stomach, shoulders, heart space), take deep breaths, and let it pass by. You can imagine placing it in a cloud in the sky or putting it in a locked box until you are ready to dive deeper into that feeling or the experience that precipitated it (Always seek a qualified psychotherapist to help if you are in crisis.). In doing so, you unleash your own power to regulate your emotions, appreciate your environment, and live in this one singular moment, which is the *present*.

Nature provides the perfect opportunity to engage in mindfulness. More specifically, flowers are the ideal symbols of nature that can provide us with opportunities to practice this art rooted in ancient cultures. We can observe the color, shape, and the delicate nature of each petal. We can smell the sweet fragrance of flowers and hear the sound of the wind blowing the stems or the insects and birds in the air around them. Most petals are soft to the touch, although some are sharp and pointy (for example, a blue thistle). Finally, some flowers are edible, such as rose, chamomile, pansy, and violet, which can add flavor and beauty to your dish or baked item (Make sure to research this first before trying a new one!). "Stop to smell the roses" takes on a whole new meaning as you explore the depth and wisdom of being in the presence of these beautiful and magical living beings created simply for our enjoyment on this earth.

Flowers are also great models of the magic of self-care. The idea of caring for oneself in a directive and empowered manner has been around for several decades. In fact, the self-compassion movement, as described by University of Texas researcher Kristin Neff, PhD, involves the idea of treating yourself as you would a good friend—turning inward the same kindness, care, and love you would typically give to others.[2] This technique, also called a "reframe" in cognitive behavioral therapy, is the basis for becoming aware of and changing one's negative thoughts and self-critical comments into more positive, supportive statements. Doing so triggers a chain of events in which one's positive thoughts result in improved emotional responses, which, in turn, activates positive behavioral change.

Flowers and humans have some common attributes in relation to the specific types of care needed to survive and thrive. Flowers require healthy and fertile soil for root development, plenty of sunshine, thoughtful watering, positive talk, and uplifting

[2] Neff, Kristin (2015). Self-Compassion: Stop Beating Yourself Up and Leave Insecurity Behind. William Morrow Paperbacks.

messages. Humans, too, require a healthy footing on our earth (also called "grounding") and in our environment, some time spent outdoors for fresh air and vitamin D provided by the sun, daily water intake equivalent to half our body weight in ounces, and an abundant mindset with plenty of positive self-talk and self-compassion. For all living beings, consistency, nurturance, and patience are required in order for growth and development to occur over time.

This journal is divided into twelve months, and each month highlights a specific flower. The origin and meaning of each flower will be provided and questions will follow for journal prompts. Specifically, each month's theme and flower meaning are highlighted to engage you in a deeper exploration of your perspective on specific areas of your life, using positive language and supportive self-talk. I highly suggest you purchase one or more stems of that month's flower to have a richer and more tangible experience. In addition, the journal provides a space to document how well you have engaged in self-care: time spent connecting with the earth, specific outdoor activities you engaged in during the month, and documenting the ways in which you maintained your water intake.

It is my hope that this unique approach to mindfulness and self-care will allow you to experience the beauty of flowers, learn their history and unique meanings, and garner new ways of cultivating a life in full bloom.

January Flower: Carnation

The carnation flower, also known as Dianthus caryophyllus, is a type of herbaceous flowering plant native to the Mediterranean region, but it is now widely cultivated and grown all over the world.

The word "carnation" is derived from the Latin word "carnis," which means flesh or body, due to the original color of the flower being a light pink or peachy tone that resembled some colors of human flesh. However, many other colors of carnations were later cultivated. The carnation flower is regarded as a symbol of love, fascination, and distinction. It is a popular flower choice for gift giving, especially on special occasions such as birthdays or holidays such as Mother's Day or Valentine's Day.

Carnations are known for their ruffled petals and sweet fragrance, reminiscent of bubble gum or other sweet candy. They come in a wide range of colors and are long-lasting flowers that hold their shape well, making them a good option for corsages and boutonnieres for special events such as weddings and proms. Miraculously, these cut flowers can last for a couple of weeks if maintained in fresh water.

The meanings attached to carnations vary by color: Red carnations represent deep love and admiration, pink carnations symbolize gratitude and affection, and white carnations represent purity, innocence, and remembrance.

In conclusion, carnations are known for their vibrant colors, perfumed fragrance, and long-lasting nature. Their historical symbolism rooted in the Latin-derived word for "flesh" or "body" reflects their endurance and resilience, given the proper love and care.

JANUARY JOURNAL PROMPTS:

What specific things do you notice about the carnation that appeal to your senses?

Given that the carnation means "flesh" or "body," in what ways do you take care of and show gratitude for your body? Use positive, affirming words.

If you need more motivation in this area, what is one NEW way you plan to take care of your body this month? Examples could be exercising a certain number of times per week, exploring new food options for health, making a doctor appointment, or adding a new vitamin or supplement. Be *very* specific.

I plan to take care of my body by…

How will you spend time outdoors this month? How will you connect to the earth? With cold weather, this can be a bit more challenging, so be creative (Yes, shoveling snow off your driveway counts!):

How much water in ounces do you need to drink daily? Calculate half of your body weight in ounces. Use this space to make a firm commitment to drink more water, and write down a new practice to help you achieve this (example: buy a new stainless steel water bottle this month).

I will commit to drinking more water by…

Additional Seeds of Thought:

February Flower: Violet

The violet flower (whose scientific name is Viola odorata) is a small, fragrant flower that belongs to the Violaceae family. It is native to Europe and parts of Asia, but it can also be found in many other regions of the world.

The name "violet" comes from the Latin word "viola," which means "violet color." This flower has roots in various cultural and historical contexts. For example, in Greek mythology, violets were associated with the goddess Athena and were believed to offer protection and strength. In Christianity, violets are sometimes called "Our Lady's Modesty" and believed to represent the Virgin Mary's modest and pure nature. In some cultures, violets are considered flowers of remembrance and represent mourning and loss.

In the language of flowers, the violet is considered to be a symbol of modesty, humility, and faithfulness. Due to its delicate appearance and sweet scent, the violet is also thought of as a symbol of love and sentimentality. There are some variations in the purple hue of violets, and the darker purple colors have been associated with royalty and luxury.

Violet flowers have been used for various purposes throughout history. For example, in traditional medicine they were used for their medicinal properties and have also been used in cooking to add flavor and fragrance. You will often see violets as colorful accents adorning cakes or in salads (However, keep in mind they do have a laxative effect!). The subtle scent of violets is often used in perfumes, bubble baths, and skincare products.

Overall, violets are widely appreciated for their delicate beauty and sweet fragrance, and they are regarded as symbols of modesty and humility.

FEBRUARY JOURNAL PROMPTS:

What specific things do you notice about the violet that appeal to your senses?

Given that the violet means "humility" or "faithfulness," in what ways have you humbly shown up for yourself or others? Examples could include ways you give yourself "just enough" rather than overindulging (such as working on portion sizes of food or not buying new clothes or other items if not needed), and/or ways you give to others without the expectation of receiving something in return (donating to charity, volunteer work, or helping someone in need). Use positive, affirming words.

If you need more motivation in this area, what is one NEW way you plan to give yourself just enough or be available to others? Be *very* specific.

I plan to humbly show up for myself or others by…

How will you spend time outdoors this month? How will you ground? With cold weather, this can be a bit more challenging, so be creative (making a snowman counts!):

Now that you know how much water you need to drink, use this space to make a firm commitment to drink more water, and write down a new practice to help you achieve this (example: set a timer throughout the day).

I will commit to drinking more water by…

Additional Seeds of Thought:

March Flower: Daffodil

The daffodil flower, or Narcissus, is a perennial plant in the form of a bulb that belongs to the Amaryllidaceae family. It is native to Europe, North Africa, and parts of Asia, but it is widely cultivated and appreciated worldwide. This flower is known for its unique trumpet-like corona and delicate petals.

The name "daffodil" comes from the Greek mythological character Narcissus. According to this well-known legend, he became so captivated by his own reflection in a pool of water that he wasted away and transformed into the flower. The Latin name Narcissus is also derived from this myth.

Daffodils are most commonly associated with renewal, springtime, and new beginnings. They often symbolize hope, rebirth, and optimism as they are one of the first flowers to bloom in early spring, bringing cheerfulness after the long, cold, and dreary winter season. Nearly everyone has experienced that joyous feeling of seeing these vibrant yellow flowers emerge from the ground after a long winter, often signifying the arrival of spring and warmer days.

In some traditions, the daffodil represents respect and unrequited love. In others, daffodils symbolize self-esteem, independence, and individuality. Additionally, these flowers are often considered a symbol of religious or spiritual awakening and resurrection.

Overall, the daffodil flower is cherished for its brilliant color and uplifting appearance, its association with spring and new beginnings, and its ability to bring joy and optimism to those who are fortunate to witness its arrival.

MARCH JOURNAL PROMPTS:

What specific things do you notice about the daffodil that appeal to your senses?

Given that the daffodil represents optimism or rebirth, what aspect of your life do you feel could use a "rebirth?" What would your life look like if this specific aspect were different? Use positive, affirming words, as if this "rebirth" has already occurred (example: my life is filled with ease and peace as a result of…)

If you need more motivation in this area, what is one NEW actionable way you will plan for this "rebirth?" What will you do differently? Be *very* specific.

I plan to take the following action this month:

How will you spend time outdoors this month? How will you fertilize your roots? With warmer weather, this can be a lot easier: going for a walk, walking barefoot in the grass, bicycling, etc.

Use this space to continue your commitment to drinking more water, and if needed, write down a new practice to help you achieve this (example: use an online app such as MyFitnessPal to document water intake).

I will commit to drinking more water by…

____

____

____

____

____

____

____

____

____

Additional Seeds of Thought:

April Flower: Daisy

The daisy flower (whose scientific name is Bellis perennis) is an herbaceous perennial plant that belongs to the Asteraceae family. The daisy originated in Europe, but it is now widely cultivated in many regions around the world.

The name "daisy" derives from the Old English term "daes eage," meaning "day's eye," as the yellow center of the daisy resembles the sun. The typical daisy flower has a round-shaped, yellow center called a disc floret and is surrounded by white petals, referred to as ray florets.

Symbolically, daisies are often associated with innocence, purity, and simplicity. They are considered a symbol of childhood, representing hope, new beginnings, and a carefree outlook on life. Daisies are also symbols of love and romance and are often associated with the themes of loyalty, faithfulness, and everlasting affection.

In folklore and cultural traditions, daisies have held various meanings. For instance, in some traditions, it is believed that you are loved or your wish will be granted if you can blow off all the petals in a single breath. Daisies are even used in some love forecasting practices—for example, plucking the petals while repeating, "he loves me, he loves me not," alternating between the two statements until the last petal determines the answer. I remember trying this as a kid to figure out if my fourth-grade crush returned the feelings. Funny, I cannot remember the outcome of this youthful exercise that held such importance at the time.

In sum, daisies are cherished for their simple, delicate beauty, and they are also popular as a children's flower, often made into crowns or used in crafts. Overall, daisies exude a sense of purity, innocence, and optimism, as well as nostalgia.

APRIL JOURNAL PROMPTS:

What specific things do you notice about the daisy that appeal to your senses?

Given that the daisy represents youth, childhood, and nostalgia, what is a happy memory from your childhood that brings up nostalgia for you? (We are holding an awareness that some may have experienced adverse events or childhood trauma; our focus here is on even a single moment that made you smile while you were growing up.).

If you need more motivation in this area, what is one NEW actionable ritual or tradition you can implement to add that nostalgic and joyful feeling to your life this month? Or what new memories would you like to make for your current life? Be *very* specific.

I plan to take the following action this month:

How will you spend time outdoors this month? How will you ground? With April showers, this could mean walking in the rain, jumping in puddles, etc.

Have you "watered" yourself lately? Use this space to continue your commitment to drinking more water, and if needed, write down if this has been working for you or if you need to do something differently.

I will continue my commitment to "water" myself by:

Additional Seeds of Thought:

May Flower: Lily of the Valley

The Lily of the Valley flower, also known as Convallaria majalis, is a perennial plant that is native to temperate regions of the Northern Hemisphere, including Europe, North America, and Asia. The name "Lily of the Valley" derives from the Latin term "Convallaria," which means "valley." The flower was named for its tendency to grow in shady, woodland areas and because it resembles lily-shaped bells. This plant produces the tiniest, most delicate and exquisite white blossoms.

Symbolically, the Lily of the Valley is commonly regarded as a symbol of purity, humility, and sweetness. Different cultures have assigned it different meanings. For example, in the Christian tradition, it is believed that the flower represents the tears of the Virgin Mary shed during the crucifixion of Jesus.

In the language of flowers, the Lily of the Valley is often associated with sentiments such as innocence, happiness, and the return of happiness. It is a popular choice for wedding bouquets and floral arrangements, as it signifies the renewal and joy associated with marriages (Florist insider knowledge: it is also one of the most highly priced flowers, at roughly $80/bunch wholesale!).

The Lily of the Valley is one of the most sweetly fragrant flowers, and it is often used in perfumes, soaps, and other scented products. Although its delicate bell-shaped flowers are beautiful to look at, the Lily of the Valley is highly poisonous if ingested. Therefore, it should be handled with care and kept away from children and pets.

Overall, the Lily of the Valley is a cherished flower that carries deep symbolic meanings of purity, humility, and the return of happiness. Its alluring fragrance and graceful appearance make it a popular choice for various occasions and celebrations.

MAY JOURNAL PROMPTS:

What specific things do you notice about the Lily of the Valley that appeal to your senses?

Given that the Lily of the Valley is a graceful flower that represents the return of happiness, what is an area of your life in which you could give yourself more grace? Life has peaks and valleys—times where everything seems to be in sync and balanced and times when things seem chaotic or overwhelming. What would a "return" of happiness look and feel like if you allowed yourself to be relieved of any guilt feelings or negative beliefs about this issue?

If you need more motivation in this area, what is one NEW actionable way you can give yourself more grace this month? Be *very* specific. Examples include loving your body as it is and not feeling guilty when you have a sweet treat, noticing a negative thought and telling it to go away, or giving yourself permission to say “no” to someone’s request.

I plan to take the following action this month:

How will you spend time outdoors this month? How will you ground? With May flowers blooming, you might visit a botanical garden and bask in the beauty of spring!

Have you "watered" yourself lately? Nurturing your body through water is one way to show self-love—you are replenishing, restoring, and hydrating yourself, thus providing yourself much-needed energy and nourishment.

I will continue my commitment to "water" myself by:

Additional Seeds of Thought:

June Flower: Rose

The rose is one of the most iconic and popular flowers across cultures and has a rich history and symbolism. "A rose by any other name would smell as sweet." Even Shakespeare knew that no matter the name, the elegant rose was beloved by all.

The rose has also purportedly been around longer than any other flower in existence, with fossil evidence suggesting that roses have existed for at least 35 million years. It is believed that they originated in Asia, specifically in regions such as China, Persia (modern-day Iran), and the Mediterranean.

The name “rose” comes from the Latin word “rosa.” Having been cultivated originally in the Mediterranean, the flower eventually gained popularity in ancient Rome and Greece. In Greek mythology, it was linked to the goddess of love, Aphrodite, and the goddess of beauty, Venus. The rose has been associated with love, beauty, and fertility.

Historically, roses have held various symbolic meanings in different cultures. In Christianity, the rose is often associated with the Virgin Mary and can symbolize purity, divine love, and the mysteries of the Rosary. In Islamic cultures, roses are seen as symbols of paradise and divine beauty.

Although the rose has become a universally recognized symbol of love and romance, different colors of roses also carry their own meanings. For example, red roses are commonly associated with passionate love, while pink roses symbolize admiration and gratitude. White roses often represent purity and innocence, and yellow roses can symbolize friendship and joy. There are many different types of roses, including garden roses, which are hybrid roses that have a unique petal structure, exhibiting layers upon layers of tufted swirls. The Juliet Garden rose is a favorite among brides.

Many roses carry a deliciously fragrant and sweet scent, and therefore they have been used for centuries in the making of perfume. Rose water and rose oil are popular ingredients in fragrances, cosmetics, and skincare products.

Overall, the rose is a flower that carries meanings of love, beauty, and purity. The rose has been a cherished symbol worldwide due to its timeless beauty, enduring elegance, and captivating fragrance.

JUNE JOURNAL PROMPTS:

What specific things do you notice about the rose that appeal to your senses?

Given that the rose is known as a symbol of love, think of your primary relationship. What is one thing you could do to take ownership and improve your way of being in this relationship? If you are not currently in a romantic relationship, think about a past relationship and what your role was in both contributing to and perhaps taking away from its stability.

If you need more motivation in this area, what is one NEW actionable way you can improve your interactions in your (current or next) primary relationship? An example could be "I plan to take responsibility for my reactions when I am triggered and will maintain a calm voice during discussions or conflict."

I plan to take the following action this month:

How will you spend time outdoors this month? How will you connect to the earth? With June sunshine, you might plant your own garden or plant a seed in a pot and practice waiting patiently for the growth to occur.

Are you keeping up with watering yourself? One trick that some have found helpful is to fill your water bottle the night before and place it on the kitchen counter or in the refrigerator so it will be ready for you in the morning.

I will continue my commitment to "water" myself by:

Additional Seeds of Thought:

July Flower: Larkspur

The larkspur, scientifically known as delphinium, belongs to the buttercup family (Ranunculaceae) and is native to the northern hemisphere. Larkspurs are primarily found in Europe, Asia, and North America. The term "larkspur" can also refer to a specific species within the delphinium genus, namely delphinium elatum.

The larkspur is characterized by its tall, spiky stalks adorned with vibrant, spurred blossoms. Its name is derived from the shape of the flower's petals, which resemble a spur-like projection.

Symbolically, larkspur flowers are commonly associated with characteristics such as open-heartedness, positivity, and lightness of being. Because of their height, they are often seen as symbols of protection, openness, and a desire to reach for the sky.

In the language of flowers, larkspurs are often attributed with meanings such as lightheartedness, and they can represent feelings of joy, love, and affection. As with most flowers, the specific color of the larkspur petals can also influence the symbolism. For example, purple larkspurs are often associated with first love, while pink larkspurs can symbolize fickleness or the feeling of being transported elsewhere.

Larkspurs are referred to as the "birth flower" for the month of July, symbolizing joy and love. They are also associated with the zodiac sign Cancer, which captures nurturing and emotional energies.

Some herbalists believe that larkspurs have healing properties, and thus, they can be used in herbal medicine. However, it's important to note that certain parts of the plant can be toxic if ingested, so caution should be taken when handling or using them for medicinal purposes.

Overall, the larkspur flower conveys openheartedness, and its colorful blossoms and distinctive structure have made it a favorable choice for ornamental gardens and floral arrangements alike.

JULY JOURNAL PROMPTS:

What specific things do you notice about the larkspur that appeal to your senses?

Given that the larkspur symbolizes "openheartedness," think about a relationship that has been difficult lately. If you were to approach that relationship with an open heart, and even practice forgiveness, how would you respond differently to that person?

If you need more motivation in this area, what is one NEW actionable way you can improve your way of responding to someone with whom you have had a difficult relationship? Openheartedness in this case could mean that you let things go. This can be done internally through self-reflection and simply observing that this relationship has followed a trajectory which you cannot change. What you can change is how you *now* respond or think differently about the situation.

I plan to take the following action this month:

___

___

___

___

___

___

___

___

___

How will you spend time outdoors this month? How will you ground? With July temperatures rising, you might find a new swimming hole in your area or make footprints on a sandy beach (There are studies that suggest "grounding" with bare feet touching the ground is crucial for improving immunity, boosting vitality, and enhancing overall health.).

___

___

Have you "watered" yourself lately? Maintaining optimal water consumption is even more important in the summer months to avoid dehydration.

I will continue my commitment to "water" myself by:

Additional Seeds of Thought:

August Flower: Gladiolus

The gladiolus flower, also known as the sword lily, is a tall and elegant flower with an intriguing history and symbolism. The gladiolus belongs to the family Iridaceae and is native to sub-Saharan Africa, Eurasia, and some parts of the Mediterranean region.

The gladiolus gets its name from the Latin word "gladius," meaning sword, due to its sword-shaped leaves. You have probably guessed that the gladiolus has historical significance from Ancient Roman times, at which time gladiators wielded swords in grand arenas (such as the Colosseum). As a result, the gladiolus came to symbolize strength, victory, and valor.

Continuing this tradition and symbolism, in South Africa, the gladiolus is the national flower and is used to honor exceptional individuals and achievements. Throughout history, the gladiolus has also been seen as a symbol of remembrance and is sometimes used in funerals or memorial services for this reason. Its tall spires and vibrant blooms can signify stature, honor, and integrity.

In the language of flowers, gladiolus flowers can convey different meanings depending on their colors. For example, red gladiolus is often associated with love, while yellow gladiolus can symbolize friendship and joy. Pink gladiolus can convey grace and femininity, and white gladiolus is often seen as a symbol of purity and innocence.

Consistent with the month of August, Gladiolus flowers have also been associated with the zodiac signs of Leo and Virgo, representing characteristics such as strength, creativity, and practicality.

Overall, the gladiolus flower offers a unique blend of historical connections, symbolism, and aesthetic beauty. Its tall spires, with their strong and majestic presence, often provide the backbone and stability of a flower arrangement.

AUGUST JOURNAL PROMPTS:

What specific things do you notice about the gladiolus that appeal to your senses?

The gladiolus is often associated with strength, honor, and integrity. Write down one specific way that you have demonstrated these qualities in your life.

If you need more motivation in this area, what is one NEW actionable way you can demonstrate more strength, honor, and integrity in your life? An example could be admitting a mistake you made or asking for a raise at work because you have worked hard and truly deserve it.

I plan to take the following action this month:

How will you spend time outdoors this month? How will you ground? August brings continued high temperatures but also signifies the end of summer for many—this may be the last month of the summer season to enjoy your community swimming pool.

Have you "watered" yourself lately? If you have difficulty consuming water or feel it is plain and boring (as some do), you could add a hint of lemon or watermelon to spice it up.

I will continue my commitment to "water" myself by:

Additional Seeds of Thought:

September Flower: Aster

The aster flower is part of the Asteraceae family and is native to various regions around the world, including North America, Europe, and Asia. The aster is derived from the Greek word, "Astraia" meaning "star," likely because the shape of its flower head resembles a star.

In terms of symbolism, the aster flower represents love, wisdom, and affection. Due to its star-like appearance, it is often seen as a symbol of celestial energy and guidance. Asters are also associated with patience, elegance, and daintiness.

Culturally, interpretations and meanings differ for the aster flower. Ancient Romans, for example, believed aster flowers to be sacred to the gods and were associated with powerful enchantments and magical properties. According to the Victorian language of flowers, asters represented afterthought, reflection, and thinking over past events.

The aster flower blooms in many different colors, including shades of pink, purple, blue, and white. Each color carries its own symbolism. Purple asters, for example, are often associated with enchantment and royalty, while white asters represent purity and innocence. Pink asters can symbolize femininity, and blue asters are often linked with calmness and peacefulness.

In addition to their symbolic meanings, asters have various practical uses as well. These flowers are often used in gardening and landscaping as ground covers, and they have the ability to attract butterflies and pollinators. Asters are a great textural flower to add to floral bouquets and floral arrangements, providing more depth and variation.

Although the aster flower's meaning and symbolism varies across cultures, the general themes of love, wisdom, and celestial energy associated with the aster remain prevalent.

SEPTEMBER JOURNAL PROMPTS:

What specific things do you notice about the aster that appeal to your senses?

Since the aster represents celestial energy and guidance, what is your "wish upon a star?" How would your life be different if you were bestowed with the magic of the universe? Choose something that cannot be measured materially (such as a new car, new house, or other new consumer goods)—but rather, choose an internal change. Write it as if it has already happened (e.g. "I am infinitely happy and content because...").

If you need more motivation in this area, what is one NEW actionable way you can improve your life to achieve the goal above? Examples could include finding a recruiter to help look for a new job, starting a creative hobby, or joining a book club to meet new people.

I plan to take the following action this month:

How will you spend time outdoors this month? How will you solidify your footing on the earth? September may bring fall breezes, and the "back to school" vibe may mean walking your child to school or walking your dog on a new path.

How is your "watering" going? In order to remember to drink more water when temperatures get cooler, you may want to align your water consumption with the top of the hour (For example, it's 10 a.m., time to take a gulp!).

I will continue my commitment to "water" myself by:

Additional Seeds of Thought:

October Flower: Marigold

The marigold, also known as Tagetes, is native to the Americas, particularly Mexico and Central America. It has been cultivated for thousands of years and has a long history of use in traditional medicine and rituals.

In terms of symbolism, the marigold has diverse meanings across cultures. In Mexican culture, marigolds are used to decorate altars and graves as a way to honor and remember deceased loved ones during the Day of the Dead ("Dia de los Muertos") celebration.

In this context, marigolds are believed to guide the souls of the departed and bring them back to the world of the living. Marigolds are also believed to have a strong scent that attracts the spirits' attention (The scent is a bit more pungent rather than sweet.).

In other cultures, marigolds hold different meanings. In some parts of Asia, marigolds are associated with prosperity, wealth, and good luck. They are often used in religious ceremonies and as offerings to deities. In Hindu culture, marigolds are offered to deities during religious festivals and rituals (such as Lakshmi, the goddess of wealth and prosperity).

Furthermore, marigolds are often seen as a symbol of warmth, happiness, and optimism. Their bright and vibrant petals are reminiscent of sunshine, and they are commonly associated with joy and positive energy.

The marigold flower also has practical uses beyond symbolism. Marigolds are used to deter insects and pests in gardens (because of their strong scent). Additionally, marigold flowers and leaves have been used in traditional medicine for various purposes, such as treating digestive issues and skin conditions. Again, make sure to do some research before consuming any flower.

In conclusion, the marigold flower has a rich cultural history and holds different meanings depending on the context and culture. Whether it is used to honor the departed, bring good luck, or symbolize happiness, marigolds are universally inspirational with their vibrant colors and uplifting qualities.

OCTOBER JOURNAL PROMPTS:

What specific things do you notice about the marigold that appeal to your senses?

The marigold can be seen as a symbol of warmth and spirituality. Regardless of your personal religious beliefs, spirituality can take many forms. What is one way that you would like to nurture your spirituality?

If you need more motivation in this area, what is one NEW actionable way you can devote more energy to your spiritual life? Examples could include attending a religious service, reading a spiritual book, or trying a new spiritual practice such as meditation.

I plan to take the following action this month:

How will you spend time outdoors this month? How will you stay rooted and grounded? October brings cool breezes and falling leaves in many regions—noticing the colors and scents of fall can be intoxicating. Do you remember raking piles of leaves as a kid followed by the exhilarating feeling of jumping into them? You are never too old to enjoy that experience.

Hopefully you are remembering to "water" yourself. Instead of that pumpkin spice latte, opt for a cool glass of water instead.

I will continue my commitment to "water" myself by:

Additional Seeds of Thought:

November Flower: Chrysanthemum

The chrysanthemum, also called a "mum," holds great significance in Asian cultures. It is believed to have originated in China, where it has been cultivated for over 2,500 years. In ancient Chinese culture, the mum is regarded as the national flower of the country. The Chinese name for chrysanthemum, "juhua," means "flower of the nine suns," referencing a mythical creature that had nine suns.

In Japan, where the chrysanthemum is the official Imperial Seal and represents the Japanese imperial family, it is a symbol of the country itself. The Chrysanthemum Throne is the name given to the Japanese Emperor's position, emphasizing its importance in their culture. This flower is commonly used in festivals and ceremonies during the fall season, particularly in East Asia.

The chrysanthemum contains many petals and comes in a variety of colors, ranging from deep red to vibrant yellow and white. The mum is often associated with happiness, optimism, and uplifting energy. The flower's ability to bloom late in the year (typically in the fall) when other plants start to wither and fade gives it a sense of resilience, hope, and longevity.

Interestingly, some cultures also associate the chrysanthemum with mourning and death, possibly due to its late blooming nature when other flowers are fading. In Western cultures, the chrysanthemum is widely regarded as a symbol of positivity and joy. In some US states, since the early 1900's, the "homecoming mum" was given traditionally by a boy to his homecoming date as a token of affection (pinned to a girl's clothing). These days, high school students will wear a mum (typically an artificial flower) to school on the day of the homecoming football game.

The chrysanthemum has been used in traditional Chinese and Japanese medicine for centuries due to its medicinal properties. It is believed to have various healing properties, including antioxidant, anti-inflammatory, and antibacterial effects.

In conclusion, the chrysanthemum is popular in East Asian cultures as well as in Western traditions and is associated with good health, longevity, and joy.

NOVEMBER JOURNAL PROMPTS:

What specific things do you notice about the chrysanthemum that appeal to your senses?

The chrysanthemum is often associated with longevity and good health. What is one way you can improve your health and longevity? Remember that you are valued and loved, and you deserve to be healthy and happy.

If you need more motivation in this area, what is one NEW actionable way you can improve your health and life span? Examples could include stopping an unhealthy habit such as smoking or vaping, drinking less alcohol, adding a healthy habit such as exercise, or trying a new healthy recipe book.

I plan to take the following action this month:

How will you spend time outdoors this month? How will you ground? With November temperatures cooling, you can still get outside for a walk—grab your favorite hat and scarf, and bundle up!

Have you "watered" yourself lately? Cold months can mean you do not feel like drinking as many cool drinks. You can drink water at room temperature or try a new herbal tea (Yes, tea counts as long as it does not include excess sugar.).

I will continue my commitment to "water" myself by:

Additional Seeds of Thought:

December Flower: Ranunculus

Although the holly or the narcissus are commonly known as December birth flowers, we are choosing to highlight the ranunculus this month as a beloved flower that has universal appeal to everyone and is not tied to any one cultural or religious celebration.

The ranunculus flower, also commonly known as the buttercup, is a genus of about 600 species of flowering plants believed to have originated in Asia. This unique and magical flower has now been cultivated and harvested in many other parts of the world such as Europe and North America.

The word "ranunculus" itself is derived from the Latin word "rānunculus," which means "little frog." The flower often grows near water, similar to the habitat of frogs. Frogs are known to be playful, "bouncy," and prolific, and the ranunculus is no different.

In terms of meaning and symbolism, the ranunculus has numerous tiers of petals that symbolize layers of personality and depth. Other common associations with the ranunculus include charm, attractiveness, radiant beauty, and being rich in complexity. It comes in many vibrant colors, including white, yellow, orange, peach, pink, and red.

In some cultures, the ranunculus flower is also considered a symbol of rebirth and new beginnings. The ranunculus is grown from a bulb which remains dormant throughout winter and then emerges in the spring, representing the start of a new season or a fresh start in life. Additionally, the ranunculus flower is associated with love and affection, and it is a popular choice for floral arrangements and weddings.

Overall, the ranunculus is a beautiful and uniquely layered flower that is generally regarded as a symbol of beauty, love, charm, playfulness, and the potential for growth and renewal.

DECEMBER JOURNAL PROMPTS:

What specific things do you notice about the ranunculus that appeal to your senses?

The ranunculus is often associated with complexity and depth, as well as playfulness. December is the perfect month to review the year, what you have accomplished, and how you would like the next year to look and feel. Humans are complex beings, and change often occurs layer by layer, step by step. What is one positive change you have achieved in the past year, even one small incremental step towards your goal?

How can you add more playfulness to your life next year? If you need more motivation in this area, what is one NEW actionable way you can have more fun in the coming year? Examples could include playing more games with family, playing a sport (such as pickleball), going to a comedy show, or traveling to a new place.

I plan to take the following action this month (or year):

How will you spend time outdoors this month? How will you continue to fertilize your roots? December is a great month for holiday strolls, snowball fights, and ice-skating.

Have you kept up with your water intake? When it's cold outside, sometimes a hot chocolate really hits the spot! While a warm cocoa can soothe the soul, continuing your water intake is still super important in the winter so you have extra energy to get up and move your body.

I will continue my commitment to "water" myself by:

Additional Seeds of Thought:

About the Author

Andrea Zeddies is a psychologist who discovered a passion for flowers. She has a doctorate in Counseling Psychology from the University of Texas at Austin and a Master's in Marriage, Family, and Child Counseling from the University of San Diego. Dr. Zeddies maintains a part-time private practice in Austin specializing in autism evaluations and assessment of developmental disabilities, aptitude, learning disabilities, and behavioral disorders, as well as psychotherapy with a focus on parenting and women's issues. She is also a certified Mindfulness instructor. As a way of balancing her clinical work, Dr. Zeddies began her floral education in 2017 and never looked back! Her floral design company, Wildflower Rx, is the perfect union of flowers and emotions, resulting in a prescription for happiness. When she is not immersed in her work, Dr. Zeddies enjoys spending time with her husband, their three daughters, and their dogs and cats.